AF251685

The
Arguably
Immoral
Agenda
Of
The
Reverend
R.I.
Twinger

Also by W.T. Jeffrey

Literature:

The Earthist: Musings in Postmodern Pagan
Thought

A Kentucky Tale

What's God Got to Do with It?

Music:

Rock Camp Blues

Available at
Glenreynie.com

Library of Congress Control Number: 2015952335

ISBN: 978-0-9862994-2-1

Published by
Glenreynie
946 Rock Camp Branch Road
Vanceburg, Kentucky 41179
www.glenreynie.com

The Arguably Immoral Agenda Of The Reverend R.I. Twinger

By W.T. Jeffrey

GLENREYNIE
VANCEBURG, KENTUCKY

Welcome to another edition of
Common Sense!

I'm your host:
Paine Thomas

Tonight's guest is Reverend R.I. Twinger. Rev. Twinger has just released his new book "Right is Right is Right, Unless It's Wrong." Rev. Twinger, welcome and thanks for being on the show.

"Well Paine I'm certainly glad to be here and I always rejoice at the chance to get the word out."

Rev. Twinger when you say "get the word out" you are not just talking about your book, you really mean "the word" as a metaphor for your religious views. Is that correct?

"Yes, Paine, not sure what you mean by metaphor, I just say it straight up like it is. And I don't really have religious views. That sounds like opinions. One either knows the truth or not, and God's word is the only truth."

In your book the bible is always right and pretty much everything else is wrong. You suggest everything a person needs to live a meaningful and morally correct life is in the bible. Anything else is either useless or a distraction from the narrow path to salvation. This seems a bit extreme. I mean what about music, art, education, science, medicine, literature?

"Well it is like this. The bible is our road map. It shows us the right way through life. At times we can know things that are in the mind of God but not in the bible, things that can make life better like cars or computers or medicines. Sometimes God's spirit inspires us to make music or paint paintings or write stories that glorify God's presence in our lives. But make no mistake about it, you've got to keep that bible roadmap in front of you at all times or you'll get lost."

You state several times in your book that the bible is the "Word of God," totally inspired by God, without error or contradiction, is literally true and should be taken literally. You also state that the King James Version of the bible is the only acceptable translation. Why exactly is that and where does this claim about the bible's inspiration originate? Is there a passage or some specific verse in the bible that requires one to believe the whole thing is as you say? And you will have to forgive me. If I quote from scripture tonight I'll use the more scholarly NRSV since I'm not an expert in Shakespearean English.

"The King James is the authorized version. It was the first perfectly and most completely translated English version, and what they had right then is right now. A lot of people don't like what the bible says, and ever since people been trying to change it. We don't hold for none of that business. Now in Timothy it says that the scriptures are inspired by God and suitable for everything we need, and that about sums it up."

Out of curiosity Reverend, do you by chance read the biblical languages, Hebrew, Greek?

"No sir, I don't see that as necessary. We have an inspired and authorized version in our own good English, and that's good enough. I will look words up sometimes to add a little something to sermons, a little gravy for the grits you know, but one has to be careful. It says quite clearly not to test God. A person who digs around too much is asking for trouble."

So for example, when we look at the Timothy passage you referenced and find that it is ambiguous, that it seems to differentiate between various scriptures, suggesting some are "God-breathed" and useful for teaching, etc., but not necessarily "all," that doesn't bother you? And what about other passages where the title "Word of God" is applied directly to the person of Jesus and not scripture? Isn't that sort of manipulating the texts to conform to your ideology?

"No Paine, that's what we call straining out a gnat and swallowing a camel."

Ok. So this reliance upon King James, I mean you do realize when the title page says "Authorized Version" that's only alluding to the approval of the king of England. I assume you know that the version you are reading now isn't exactly the 1607 version. So what about all the discoveries since the 17th century of biblical manuscripts, fragments of manuscripts, the Dead Sea Scrolls, other writings and libraries that give modern scholars a much bigger picture for translating the bible today? Shouldn't these things be taken into consideration if you want to really know as much as you can about the bible?

"Well no Paine inspired is inspired, and it stays as it lays."

As an American you don't have a problem with an English king who reigned less than 200 years from the American Revolution commanding into existence what would become, at least for English speaking peoples, "the word of God?"

"Well in the book of Romans it says God puts government leaders in their high place. We also can judge by one's fruits. So when you consider that King James gave us this great English translation of the bible, it speaks for itself."

So you believe every leader of every government is there by God's will. There have been some pretty horrible rulers throughout history. Hitler for one, I mean what kind of a god raises up a maniac like that?

"Paine, every person including rulers choose whether to obey God or not. It's not God's fault people do wicked things, and sometimes like with Pharaoh in the bible God hardens their hearts and condemns them in their iniquity."

Seems like an awful lot of innocent people end up suffering for what ought to be a preventable scenario in the first place. God is supposed to be omniscient, right? Why would God want to allow people to rise in power that are going to bring about calamity, corruption, and harm to the world? This seems malevolent or at least grossly irresponsible and indifferent to human life.

"No one can fathom the depth of God's wisdom or stand in judgment of his will. Everything he does and the reason for it is in the divine plan and for all things we give God the glory."

OK then, what about President Barack Obama? By your beliefs his election to the US presidency, twice, had to be in God's plan. He has led the recovery of the US economy. He's worked to resolve the wars created by the Bush administration. President Obama has sought just immigration reform and health care for many Americans who were suffering without access to health insurance. He professes to be a Christian. Yet from the first moment he was elected, even before he took office, Republicans, especially those like you with fundamentalist Christian beliefs have opposed him, attempted to thwart most everything he's tried to accomplish, and have been adamant in the determination to see him fail. Isn't this a contradiction in your faith? Why not accept his election as God's will and give him the benefit of the doubt, work with him for the good of the American people?

"It's not that simple. He's the most liberal president we've ever had. He's pro-Muslim, pro-Gay, pro-abortion, anti-gun, anti-Israel, and we still don't know he's even an American citizen. Shoot Paine, just look at his name. That ain't no American name. Contrary to what people say sometimes you do well to judge a book by its cover."

All right, last comment aside let's break that down. The phrase in the Declaration of Independence "Life, Liberty, and the Pursuit of Happiness" has been a core value for Americans from pretty much the beginning of our country. It would seem to imply that being liberal is essential if we are going to respect the rights and choices of others. Why is the word liberal such a problem?

"Well Paine, it is several things. First if someone is choosing to live a sinful, un-American, and un-Christian life then liberal is basically a license to sin. We can't have that. That's exactly what brings God's judgment on our country. You can't have life, liberty, and happiness if you are not following the Lord Jesus Christ. Like the saying 'You can lead a horse to water, but you can't make him drink,' we can't make everybody serve God, but we don't have to sit back and let sin take over. And second, liberals like Obama want the government to do everything, run everything, be in everyone's business, and worse, force sin on everybody."

There are a lot of people in this country....

"Now that's a problem too."

Not everyone is Christian. What about Jews, Muslims, Native Americans that hold to ancient traditions, Buddhists, and people that reject religion as myth and superstition? There is a pretty long list of people who disagree with Christianity and even within Christianity there is a lot of disagreement over what it means to be Christian.

"Paine, America was founded as a Christian nation. We tolerate sinners in the hopes they'll see the truth and be saved. But under no circumstances should these people have a place in government. If they don't like living by God's word and the authority of godly leaders they can pack up and leave. And anyone who calls himself a Christian and doesn't obey the bible is a liar and a fool."

So from your perspective, your interpretation of your religion, it's 'my way or the highway.'

"Well Paine what's right is right is right."

Or as you also say "unless it's wrong." So was Thomas Jefferson a Christian? He was obviously very influential among the founders of the United States.

"All of the founding fathers were Christians."

Have you ever read Jefferson's translation of the gospels? He didn't believe in miracles, the virgin birth, or even the resurrection so he edited them out. He also wrote rather poignantly about separation of church and state.

"No Paine, I see no point in reading garbage like that. When these great men put pen to the page they were Christians because God was inspiring them to create a Christian nation. If any of them fell into error later on, then they'll answer to God for it."

Ok. When you were talking about President Obama and liberals you made the statement they were pro-abortion, pro-gay, anti-gun, etc. Many liberals take offense at these generalizations. For example there are a lot of people who believe women have the right to make their own personal and private choices regarding reproduction including the termination of a pregnancy. Likewise a lot of people and not exclusive to GLBT persons believe all citizens deserve equal treatment under the law. In other words it would seem more accurate to say pro-constitution than pro-gay. And as far as guns, given the horrendous gun violence in our country, isn't it reasonable to seek ways to address this problem. My question though is this. The conservative Christian platform has been beating these issues like a dead horse for about three decades. For the most part these issues end up being decided by the Supreme Court because regardless of legislative action in any particular state it is constitutional law that's going to apply. Can't we move on?

"Absolutely not, Paine. We're going to take this country back for Jesus Christ. We have the House and the Senate, and soon we'll have the Oval Office. Next we'll have the Supreme Court, and we will see a revival of righteousness in the land like never before. We'll overturn every liberal activist decision and purge the sin from sea to shining sea, hallelujah! And when Jesus comes he'll find this house swept clean."

Rev. Twinger you accused President Obama of being anti-Israel, why is that? Our government through as many administrations as I can remember has supported Israel. They are our strongest ally in the Middle East. Likewise we have worked diligently to find solutions that will bring peace between Israelis and Palestinians as well as to the broader region. The Islamic wars and conflicts taking place now represent perhaps the greatest foreign policy crisis that we and many other nations have ever faced. Obviously the role of Israel is very important. So what exactly is it about Israel that you see as the problem here?

"Paine, you may not understand, but this isn't just about politics. Even though Christians are the only people who are truly saved, still the Jews hold a special place in God's plan. God's promise to them goes all the way back to Abraham. They were His chosen people, and through them the world was given Jesus Christ. The bible is clear about this and in the book of Revelation they play an important role in the second coming of Christ. Bible prophecy, especially the books of Daniel and Revelation, make it very clear that the end times are upon us, and this makes our relationship to Israel very important. We cannot afford to have a president who treats Palestinian Muslims with privilege at the expense of Israel."

So you are saying one of your motives in electing the president of the United States is to have someone in office who will conduct America's foreign policy in conjunction with what fundamentalist Christians consider biblical prophesies, a president that will show preferential treatment to Israel because of the bible.

"Yes, Paine. Right now Israel is the most important nation in the world and to turn our back on her is like a slap in God's face. Jesus is coming, as well as years of tribulation, and the time of Armageddon. Blessed is the nation whose God is the Lord. We must have a Christian at our helm that understands these things."

I'm surprised the fact that Israel has legalized abortion and universal health care for its citizens isn't a drawback for the conservative Christian agenda.

"Only Jesus is perfect, Paine. Many Jews may yet accept Christ. They too will be judged, but it is the Holy Land, emphasis upon land, God's chosen Promised Land that matters."

Well Rev. Twinger thanks for the those points of clarification. Let's move on to some of the other things you say in your book. You indicate you are very pleased with rising number of Republican candidates and the fact that so many are conservative minded Christians like yourself. Personally I've lost track there is so many. Let's see there's Huckabee, Cruz, Bush, Graham, Jindal, Trump, but he doesn't seem very religious, Paul, though the Ayn Rand thing is kind of hanging there, Rubio, Santeria…

"I believe that is Santorum."

Whatever. And there's a bunch more. Several of these candidates wave the bible around as an authority they believe is more important than even the constitution of the United States. Some have gone as far to say the bible is a higher moral authority than rule of law, that essentially it trumps everything. Could you elaborate on this and talk about what you think can be accomplished given that the first amendment prohibits the government from making laws respecting an establishment of religion?

"Well first there are many of us who correctly interpret the first amendment to mean that the government cannot tell churches what to do but it does not say that the church cannot have a role in governance. It is incorrect that this amendment separates church and state, so it is quite appropriate to legislate Christian values."

Well but the government can't limit the free exercise of religion either. That means any religion or even secular perspectives that for those who hold them are the equivalent of a religion are protected. To pass an inherently Christian law is going to infringe on the rights of other religions. Any way you cut it you are going to end up with separation of church and state. Further it is quite clear that Jefferson, Madison, and others saw this very first statement in the Bill of Rights as a guarantee that the government would not establish a national religion. But you are serious about seeing the bible used as an authority in American law?

"Yes Paine, absolutely."

So is that the New Testament, Old Testament? I mean it has been very popular for Christians to use verses from the Old Testament when it suited a particular cause, even though the apostle Paul states Christians are not under the Law. So what exactly is the standard for what's in or what's out?

"Paine, the bible, the whole bible is the word of God. If we want to be a righteous nation the whole thing applies. Everyone from our legislators to our judges to our school officials needs to have the bible and its teachings close at hand."

Fair enough reverend, but honestly aren't there some aspects of the bible that pretty much all of us in modern times consider passé? For example, in the Ten Commandments it says "Thou shall not covet." To covet means to ardently desire something that someone else has. Obviously such things as greed, envy, and jealousy can be morally problematic. Yet our whole economy, free market capitalism, is based

upon inciting people to covet. The goal of advertizing
is to make people want something, and frequently the
way to do that is to depict someone else having or
enjoying something you don't have. And if I'm not
mistaken the whole foundation of the prosperity
gospel which is a very popular movement within
fundamentalist Christianity is to court the desires of
people who want more for themselves. The mantra is
"give us money and God will bless you." In turn
people drool over the opulence of the Creflo Dollar's
and Kenneth Copeland's and think they're going to
enjoy a similar success. It would seem by and large
people endorse the sales pitch and are willing to risk
being hoodwinked as long as they have a chance to
get the goods others are flaunting. "Thou shall not
covet" has changed to "Caveat Emptor," and this, so
it would appear, by a broad consensus around what is
normative for our time.

"Well Paine I think you misunderstand
prosperity. It is God who desires for his people to
enjoy the foretastes of his heavenly promise. Not all
covetousness is wrong, only that desire which is
contrary to God's will is sin. The word of God makes
this clear. The bible is the true gold standard, and
neither a jot nor a tittle of it is passé."

Reverend Twinger when you say the bible is the
word of God and insist it should be taken at face
value as the ultimate source of authority isn't it fair
for the rest of us in society to examine it objectively, to
test it for credibility?

"Well Paine everyone should read it and believe it. Keep in mind though that God demands we accept his will through faith. I don't know what value there is in testing it except maybe for someone to find out how little he knows about the truth."

Most people aren't that gullible. It is fair to require evidence. Because someone says something is so doesn't make it so. You want to govern people, determine what people can and can't do, based upon a book that you claim is divine so it seems fair to test your claims against what can be known about the bible. And frankly, the bible contains contradictions. You say the whole thing was inspired, but there are even passages where the writer credits another source for his material. Come on, even you can see how these problems diminish credibility.

"Paine, there are no contradictions in the bible. Some things are mysterious and difficult for those without faith to understand. If it is written in the Word it is the truth, it is fact, and people will do well to see it that way."

Ok. Look at the resurrection of Jesus. Mark's ending is fragmented so it can be set aside. Matthew has Jesus going to Galilee to bid farewell to his disciples and even says not all of the disciples believed his final appearance was real. Luke says it all happens in Jerusalem with a whole bunch more appearances to his disciples and no trip to Galilee. John has him being crucified on a different day than the other three gospels. He has Jesus in Jerusalem making appearances for more than a week, and then ends up with Jesus popping in once more when his disciples were back fishing in Galilee. Reverend Twinger, it strains credulity to take these stories as factual. They can't all be true which gives one pause to doubt the authenticity of any of them.

"Paine, with God all things are possible. These stories when preached correctly say exactly the same thing."

If you say so. Still it seems fair to require some evidence that God actually exists. When put to the test the bible fails to measure up to the kinds of claims you make about it.

"Paine, that's simply not true. The bible never fails to measure up. Now people fail to measure up. We're all born in sin, and without Jesus Christ as our savior we are incapable of understanding the bible correctly. Right there in Genesis it tells us we are born into sin."

Actually I'd like to challenge you on that. I mean isn't it Paul and maybe some Jewish rabbis that initially suggests the thing with Adam and Eve as a matter of free will brought sin into the world? Unless I'm mistaken the story in Genesis never mentions sin. There they are in the garden. They can eat from every tree save one, the tree of the knowledge of good and evil. They are told if they do they will surely die. The serpent, the talking serpent, tells Eve she won't die if she eats the fruit. And technically in the defense of snakes that have forever since gotten a bad rap, it wasn't a lie. She eats, doesn't die. Adam eats, doesn't die. Their eyes are opened, so to speak, and they appear to now have knowledge. God catches on because he sees them hiding their nudity which wasn't an issue before. He curses them for not obeying his command to not eat from that tree, but still no one dies. Then comes the confab where God goes and talks to the other divines and says "whoops" if the mortals now keep eating from the tree of life they'll be like us and possibly our rivals. So he kicks them out of the garden. It is only because they can no longer eat from the tree of life they are destined to die.

"Paine, it is still sin."

Let me ask you this, if God is immortal why would he need a tree, a magic plant, fruit? And who exactly is he talking to in the confab?

Well obviously the tree was for Adam and Eve so they could have youth and longevity while they faithfully served the lord. And the conversation had to be the Father, Son, and Holy Spirit."

So God was talking to himself.

"Paine it is hard for some people to understand."

Out of curiosity have you ever read the Epic of Gilgamesh, ancient Babylonian writings that predate the Hebrew Scriptures by about a thousand years? I

mean there is a magic plant and snake story there too
where mortals lose the chance for immortality. Or
perhaps you've read some of the ancient Canaanite
stuff about the god El and his sons?

"Why would I or why would I care?"

Well it does kind of crop up in the bible. El is the
ancient Israelite god too and the sons of El are
mentioned in the flood story, you know having sex
with mortal women, kind of the initial reason God
chose to deluge the world.

"I have no idea what you are talking about."

I didn't think so.

"Look Paine, I think this regression into
nitpicking is taking us away from the important point
that we are sinners. The true heroes are the ones who
preach the word of salvation, the Billy Graham's of
the world, and if you want evidence, there you go.
Just look at the hundreds, even thousands, who come
forward to be saved when they hear the word."

You're suggesting that crusades led by Billy and
Franklin Graham and I suppose even yourself
constitute evidence that a supernatural force is at
work?

"Well I don't personally do crusades, though I'm
known to preach quite fervently in the church. But
yes, God moves people's hearts and they respond.

What else can explain the great number of people over the years that have come forward to accept Jesus Christ as their personal lord and savior?"

I can think of a lot of things none of which are divine and some was it not for the constitution protecting religion would probably be considered fraud.

"Paine, that is ridiculous. No one has ever done more for the Lord than Billy Graham. His son Franklin is following in his footsteps, and frankly they are beyond reproach."

With all due respect reverend isn't that a bit naïve? The Grahams have built a multi-million dollar institution over the years. They have garnered for themselves significant status and enjoy a lot of power and influence in the Evangelical wing of the Republican Party. Billy Graham's book sales alone have brought great wealth to the family.

"Some people call that blessed."

Well, Ok. Let's look at those crusades the Grahams used to build a veritable empire. These were big events usually in large cities where substantive populations could be reached. Area churches were solicited to provide logistical support, volunteers to be trained by the Graham team, and financing. One major benefit to these churches for their investment was to receive names and addresses of people who came forward at the crusade.

"What's wrong with that Paine? Our mission is to preach the gospel and fill pews. Crusades and revival meetings have always been a great way to reach backsliders and those without a church."

There is a lot of strategy that goes into these events, so much so one could easily ask what's God got to do with it? Volunteers from churches are trained as counselors, ushers, etc. You see them as the ones wearing name tags during the altar call. In fact if you look closely at the crowd of the hundreds or even a thousand or two up front, there's an awful lot of name tags. The point is these people are trained to sit throughout the arena and during the "Just As I Am" invitation that goes on for twenty minutes they are supposed to randomly come forward. They make it look like they are moved to do this so people around them will be encouraged to follow them.

"Paine, the sheep need a shepherd."

Come on Rev. Twinger, people are sitting there being reminded of all their faults, every ounce of guilt exacerbated into a frenzy of emotion, while Billy Graham chides the audience with images of hellfire and impending doom if they do not respond. "Do you know Jesus as your personal savior? If you die tonight are you ready to meet him. Is your place in heaven secure?" How is this anything less than preying on people's fears in order to manipulate a response?

"Paine, we believe you are going to hell if you are not saved. Sometimes scaring the hell out of people is what it takes. When people are confronted with the truth they have to choose."

So I'm sitting there in the audience feeling the weight of the guilt trip, very conflicted. Part of me is considering going up front, but another part me is sensing the manipulation that is taking place. Then a person near me goes up and then another. The Grahams are professional manipulators. They know the average person will prefer to blend in so they seed the audience with volunteers to help provide that necessary nudge. This is psychological trickery on a group scale, a ploy that is proven to work for influencing group behavior.

"Well Paine we call it evangelism. The apostle Paul said 'I become all things to all people in order that I might save some.' And even though a lot of those people up there are volunteers you still see the joy and the tears of those who accepted Christ."

Yeah that's right after the "sinner's prayer." Is that in the bible?

"What do you mean?"

I mean did Jesus or Paul or any New Testament writer give a magical prayer for people to say so they could know they have been saved?

"Well the bible tells us how to be saved, Paine."

But there is no "sinner's prayer," right? Once again there are conflicting passages, passages that involve baptisms, various degrees of belief, and in some case the altering of one's behavior like caring for the needy or giving up one's possessions. Come on reverend the church has been arguing over who is saved and who isn't for centuries.

"We use the 'sinner's prayer' as a beginning. A person is given the words that initiate repentance and they confess Jesus as lord, accepting him as their personal savior. This is consistent with what the bible says has to happen."

So a person is subjected to a long sermon, typically one that is heavy on fundamentalist values, laced with endearing stories, and led to an almost endless invitation designed to heighten guilt and prey on one's vulnerability. Then in the moment of "personal" decision hundreds of volunteers are interspersed throughout the crowd to, shall we say, prime the pump. In emotional duress people go forward where they're applauded by Rev. Graham, given the words to say, and are then told they are saved to resounding approval from the crowd. Their angst is now relieved by the flow of adrenaline, serotonin, and oxytocin being released by their brain. In this moment of "joy and tears" they are led by the volunteers to an area where they can give their names and information and be encouraged to attend one of the host churches. While this may be a brilliant and highly successful strategy for influencing social behavior toward a desired outcome, sorry Rev. Twinger, it is hardly evidence for supernatural activity. In fact, if anything, it is proof to the contrary and an arguably questionable tactic on ethical grounds.

"Paine, I couldn't disagree more. I'm sure you've heard the saying 'All is fair in love and war,' and we are at war with sin."

Have you ever considered that there is really no such thing as sin? As humans we make mistakes, struggle between our carnal instincts and our evolved capacity for such things as empathy or reason. Good and evil are concepts that have been negotiated over thousands of years of human behavior which have lead us to enact rules, norms, laws that make civilization possible. There are a lot of people who reject the idea that we are born sinners and as such have no need for saviors. More and more people recognize that personal responsibility and being accountable to a larger community is the crux of what we call morality. Isn't there an absurdity in teaching people they are sinners, something inherently demoralizing especially to children, and that the only remedy for this condition is belief in a human sacrifice?

"Paine, I don't think it is at all appropriate to speak of Jesus that way. His sacrifice wasn't a human sacrifice; it was God's plan to atone for our sins. "

Well he was a human and his purpose in life was to die a sacrificial death. Sacrificing a virgin to appease the gods is an old motif. In any other context it would be considered barbaric. It is not even appropriate for religions to do animal sacrifices in the United States, yet crucifixes abound.

"The blood of Jesus is what brings us forgiveness for our sins and makes it possible for us to be welcomed as God's children. Paul said the cross would be foolishness to those who disbelieve, but the wisdom and power of God for the faithful. Also I would point out that it is God's word that reveals God's will and there is no greater morality than that."

Well reverend the whole cross debacle does come across as foolishness to a lot of people. Aside from the barbaric and primitive notion that a bloody, gory sacrifice somehow appeals to a divine being is the premise that a god who could create a universe as complex as ours would require animal sacrifices and later the sacrifice of a human being in order to forgive people. It has been argued by many that a god that would create humans in his image, leave them vulnerable to unbearable suffering, punish them for not loving him for it, and use crucifixion as a means to salvation is not only capricious and flippant, but grossly callous and malevolent.

"Paine I hardly think it is appropriate for the creature to judge its creator. Those of us that are true Christians know God is good and right in all things. His will cannot be challenged or changed. That's why it is our duty to lead America to Christ and see to it that our nation is a Christian nation."

So it is not good enough for you to be protected under the constitution so that you can practice your religion without infringement and hold your private beliefs without persecution?

"No it truly is not. What's right is right is right unless it is wrong. Christianity is right and all other religions and philosophies are wrong. Maybe tolerance has its place, maybe. If other people want to risk eternal hellfire that's their choice, but they have no right to take the rest of us with them. As I've said the bible is above all else and should be the centerpiece of our government, our schools, and our society."

If you would, talk a little bit about the Christian right wing's movement over the last few decades to take over the government.

"I'm not sure what you mean, Paine."

Well we've already touched on Billy Graham and now his son Franklin. But going back to the days of Jerry Falwell and the Moral Majority, followed by the Christian Coalition which was firmly rooted in the south, then ministries like Pat Robertson's 700 Club, James Dobson's Focus on the family, and the swelling number of Christian lobby groups, there has been an overt, intentional, and quite outspoken movement to elect Christian evangelicals and fundamentalists to government offices. Do you deny that?

"No I don't deny that. We want godly people who agree with us on every level of government from local governments and school boards all the way to the White House. Some have argued that this violates the separation between church and state, but we don't care. Even the IRS won't challenge us on this."

You mean because you persist in violating the terms of the 501 c.3 section of the law code which grants tax exempt status to religious organizations but stipulates you can't actively engage in politics. Things like endorsing political candidates or holding political rallies in churches are illegal.

"We don't care because they shouldn't be. The government has no right to make laws respecting an establishment of religion, and I believe if the IRS ever pursues it they will lose. So we will endorse candidates and hold meetings in our churches that set forth the platform we believe will make America a Christian nation. We're going to end abortion, eliminate rights for homosexuals, remove evolution from our schools, and restore the bible to its rightful place."

Do you believe that making abortions illegal ends abortion?

"It comes pretty close to it, Paine."

Women had abortions before 1973, reverend. Wealthy and middle class women were always in a position to either travel to a country where it was legal, or possibly have a personal physician that would assist them. It was low income women that were reduced to back alley butchery and questionable procedures that could cause them harm or even death. Just like Prohibition didn't end alcohol consumption making abortion illegal won't stop the termination of pregnancies. It would only discriminate against lower income women. Doesn't it seem reasonable that all women should have the right to safe, quality medical care and to the privacy to make their own medical decisions?

"Not if it is an abortion."

Is abortion ever actually forbidden in the bible?

"Well God creates life, knows us all from even before we are conceived, and commanded us not to kill. Our God is a god of love. Abortion isn't love."

But these laws you quote were originally only for the ancient Israelites. The god of the bible had no problem commanding the slaughter of the men, women, children, and even infants of the cultures that surrounded the Israelites. There is a Psalm where the writer laments his captivity in Babylon, a punishment the prophets said the Lord himself brought against Israel, yet the psalmist longs for the day he can take his enemies children by the feet and dash their heads against the rocks. And for that matter in perhaps the only story that has an unwanted or unplanned child, the story of David and Bathsheba, neither of them are punished, not even David who coveted, lied, committed adultery, possibly rape, and murder. No, God's choice was to allow Bathsheba to go full term, give birth, and then take the life of the child.

"It still wasn't an abortion, and we don't question God's judgment."

So what about China?

"What about China?"

China has state sponsored abortion and has a history of some pretty serious human rights violations. Most everyone in the US does business with China and buys the goods they produce. Companies like Hobby Lobby that claim their religious rights are violated if they have to provide health care to workers that may contain benefits that allow certain types of birth control or coverage for abortion make their living selling goods imported from countries like China. How hypocritical is that?

"Paine, I hadn't really thought about it."

So it is Ok for Christians to whine about their tax dollars being used to support legal health care or programs like Planned Parenthood but what, turn the other cheek or something when it comes to voluntarily supporting similar or worse practices in other countries in order to maximize their personal incomes?

"Like I said, I hadn't really thought about it. But we all have a right to make a living. The difference is we give thanks to God, pay our tithes, and celebrate the many ways God blesses his people."

All right reverend, let's move on. Homosexuality has been a major point of conflict for conservative Christians for some time even to the point of passing amendments and laws that discriminate against same gender oriented persons. Recently the Supreme Court finally acknowledged that GLBT persons deserve equal treatment under the law. This decision voids state laws that prevent same sex marriage.

"Paine that decision was an abomination to God and proof that we must stand up against iniquity. This issue is far from over and any law that is in defiance of God's law isn't a law I'm willing to honor. Giving rights to people who choose to live in sin is yet another slap in God's face."

So you support the Rowan County Clerk in Kentucky who has defied the order to issue marriage licenses to same sex couples?

"I do, Paine. This is a violation of her religious freedom. That Kim Davis was jailed for her faith is a sign of the end times."

Many people, perhaps most, see this as a legal issue that has nothing to do with religion. She is a public servant who swore an oath to uphold the law. She was elected because of her experience not because of her faith. When the law changed and she could no longer honor her oath of office, resignation, not defiance, was the dignified choice. She has broken the law, cost Kentucky taxpayers, and discriminated against her constituents. How is this moral behavior?

"Paine, she is defending the word of God."

Reverend, she is defending an $80,000 per year salary and her son is also paid to be a deputy clerk. Resign and then go preach how hard it is to honor your convictions. Grandstanding on the public dime with the likes of Mike Huckabee fueling the flames of dissent and discrimination is for many citizens an affront to justice. A lot of people see this as taking advantage of the ignorance of Kim Davis' narrow understanding of her religion for the purpose of pandering to the prejudice and fear of fundamentalist crowds that are prone to bigotry.

"Paine, that's not at all what this is about. People who choose a homosexual lifestyle can have at it. But marriage is for a man and a woman, end of story. Kim Davis has every right to follow her conscience."

Why doesn't she resign? This isn't a religious office. It is a government job ruled by law not individual conscience. Jesus said render unto Caesar what is Caesar's, and to God what is God's. Other passages too confirm the same concept. When does the scripture give her the authority to judge others? Further, science has shown that human sexuality is a complex relationship of genetics and biology. There is no indication that people can choose their sexual orientation. They might, like heterosexuals, choose who they want to marry, but not their sexual orientation. By all rights this isn't even a religious issue. And for the record homosexuality occurs in nature in many species.

"Science, shmience. The bible is the only authority that matters."

Reverend Twinger let me ask you about something Jesus says according to Matthew's gospel. In chapter 19 the Pharisees ask Jesus about divorce. His response is very popular with fundamentalist Christians like Kim Davis. This is where he alludes to Genesis and the idea that the man and woman become one flesh and essentially should not divorce. He says divorce and remarriage is adultery unless unfaithfulness is involved though in Mark he doesn't even allow for that. Both the Pharisees and his own disciples are taken back by his teaching because it contradicts the customary tradition and the Law of Moses. His disciples say if such is the case then it is better not to marry at all. What Jesus says next is perplexing. He apparently likens himself to a person who chooses to be a eunuch, presumably one who does not marry and have a family, for the sake of the kingdom of heaven. He gives three examples of eunuchs. One I just mentioned, two the common use of the word for a male who has been castrated to serve as an attendant to female royalty, but third he says some are born eunuchs. I researched this and as it turns out the word eunuch was a common euphemism in the Greek and Roman culture for a gay man. So isn't it likely Jesus himself recognizes that some people are born with a same gender orientation? If so why doesn't he condemn them?

"Well I've never heard that before Paine. It sounds like liberal gobbledygook to me. Even if he meant that, and I doubt he did, it still doesn't condone marriage between two men or two women."

You don't read Greek or study the culture and context of these writings. You just take them at face value. What if you are wrong and GLBT persons are being dehumanized by your religious views without justification? Frankly marriage in our culture is very different than in times past. People marry because they love each other and because they want the legal protections given to the marriage union, the tax status, the inheritance rights, the rights necessary for certain aspects of medical care, and so on. Why is it so hard to accept that marriage is a private choice between two people and their sexual orientation is irrelevant?

"God defined marriage as a union between a man and a woman. God condemned homosexuality as an abomination. I'm not familiar with any verse where he says anything goes. I'd say God says what he means and means what he says."

Well we all know there is basically one verse in the Old Testament where it is a capital offense for a man to lie with a man as with a woman. It is also a capital offense for a man or woman to lie with an animal as with a human. But there is no verse that specifically forbids a woman to lie with another woman as with a man. Why do you think that is?

"I don't think it matters, Paine. The gist of it is covered and homosexuality of any kind is a sin."

God is usually pretty specific, reverend, as you say, why tell people what they can and can't eat, who they can and can't have sex with, but leave out lesbians?

"Homosexuality is a sin. It's that simple. It's common sense. God didn't have to tell people what they ought to know anyway. Right is right."

Well God specifically mentions men, and men and women in regard to animals. I think there is more to it. Of course it could be that primitive ignorance in regard to the female role in reproduction and human sexuality in general had something to do with it or it could just be the obvious.

"The obvious?"

Yes, Rev. Twinger, the obvious. Do you enjoy sex?

"Paine, that's a little personal, but of course I enjoy sex with my wife which I will point out is a pleasure God's word secures for those who are faithful in marriage."

Well according to the bible you could have many wives. In fact the primary biblical family "value" was polygamy. Of course that is now illegal in the United States for a variety of reasons, but surely you can imagine living in bible times and having more than one wife.

"I suppose I can, Paine. What's your point?"

So there you are, you have wives, their concubines, and maybe you all live in a big tent. The time comes for sex. So what do you think happens? Would you only have sex with one at a time? On occasion don't you think you would want them all to join in? I mean don't most heterosexual men fantasize about this stuff? There you are, you have four or five women who have to do what you tell them to do. Aren't you going to want to at least watch them play?

"Paine, that is disgusting. I can't believe you would even imply such a thing."

Well, reverend, it was God that failed to forbid female with female sexual relations. How fortuitous for a patriarchal culture given to misogyny and the frequent subjugation of women to the status of property.

"I can't possibly imagine such things happening in Israel, but the roles of men and women were determined by God, what it meant to be clean or unclean, what was required to be holy. God is a holy God. Our duty is to obey his word."

Perhaps you lack imagination, reverend. So about obeying his word, out of curiosity, are you circumcised?

"That's really none of your business, Paine, but I know where you are going with that. The New Testament changed that law and Christians are not required to become Jewish before accepting Christ."

So you admit that there are aspects of one part of the bible that nullify other parts of the bible?

"I don't think I'd put it that way."

Well for example the food laws in the Old Testament, persons who ate pork or shrimp were considered unclean and unacceptable before God. Are those laws you obey?

"In the New Testament there is a story involving Peter where those food laws are cancelled for Christians and also Paul points out that we are not under the Law of Moses, but Christ."

What about the kosher laws for eating meat slaughtered so that the blood has drained out a certain way? That's a big deal in the Old Testament, and I believe it is also mentioned as a requirement for Christians in the Book of Acts. Do you only eat kosher meat?

"Paine, once again you are straining out a gnat to swallow a camel."

Ok. A couple of things, I notice you have a tattoo on your arm and that you are wearing a Masonic ring. Both of those things are taboo for people who want to obey the god of the bible. I mean marking your body is forbidden in Leviticus, and if I'm not mistaken in order to join the Freemasons you have to swear an oath of secrecy and allegiance. Isn't there a place where even Jesus said no one can serve two masters?

"The problem here Paine is you are grasping for straws. Even if my tattoo was a sin, Jesus has forgiven me. And as for Freemasonry, many of our greatest leaders including George Washington were Masons. I don't expect you'd understand."

I understand that when Washington used language in his prayers like "Supreme Architect of the universe" he was using Masonic language and invoking what most would agree was a Deistic and not specifically Christian belief.

"That's not a subject we need to discuss."

Well Reverend Twinger you have to admit that it sure seems like no matter what question is raised it is always Ok for you to pick and choose the things that are irrelevant in the bible where you're concerned. Then whenever you disagree with someone else's lifestyle all of a sudden bible passages apply. Isn't that hypocrisy?

"No Paine, it is moral fortitude. Those of us who live by God's Word know the difference between what matters and what doesn't. We can go around in circles all night long but it doesn't change the fact that the bible is the foundation for all that is moral and good. We are created in the image of God, and those of us who are in Christ understand the mind of God."

Do you have any idea how condescending that sounds? What about all of the evidence that shows that we humans are a species like all other species that has evolved over millions of years? Even America with our emphasis on rule of law is a testament to the evolving progress of humanity. There are many who would argue that our laws and standards today are much more moral than the ancient laws reflected in the bible.

"Well I don't know who would argue that. And really Paine, how can any rational human being believe we came from monkeys? Evolution is a mere theory produced by morons too dumb to believe in God. When's the last time you saw a monkey become human? This is exactly the kind of crap that needs to be taken out of the schools once and for all. Besides what could be more immoral than the idea of survival of the fittest? That's just a view that promotes a godless world where anything goes for those who can get away with it."

So that is how you understand evolution?

"Is there any other way?"

Well there would be what science actually teaches about evolution. First, a theory is not a guess. It is an explanation of facts and in the case of evolution there happens to be an overwhelming body of evidence for which evolution is the best explanation. With each passing day new research continues to confirm that species including humans evolved. We share a common ancestry with other primates, but Homo sapiens are a unique species. Monkeys will evolve as will humans, but they won't become human. Survival of the fittest doesn't mean that the strongest or most ruthless prevail but that the species who best adapt and "fit in" with the changing natural world are most likely to survive. In fact contrary to the idea that a godless world means anything goes stands the evidence that we have evolved to value diversity, reciprocity, altruism, benevolence, and compassion. These things have proven beneficial to our species and we select them as a strategy integral to survival.

"The bible says God created every creature according to its kind and we were specially created in the image of God. We are who we are because God's word is instilled within us. God is love and compassion. Right off the bat, the very first thing God wanted us to know, was that he created everything, period. That should be the first thing children should learn in school not evolution."

Reverend, isn't the passage you are referring to ambiguous? You take it as a definitive statement, but translators say otherwise. It can also be read "When Elohim began to create the earth was without form and void." It is as if the writer begins with "Once upon a time" then proceeds to tell a story that leads to an explanation for why Jewish people observe the Sabbath.

"That is ridiculous, Paine. Anyway you cut it God is still the creator and the story is clearly about creation."

I don't know reverend, most all ancient cultures before science assumed gods created the world and cosmos. It seems this story like the ones that follow intend to explain something in particular like the Sabbath Day. In the next chapter there's a different creation story which is virtually identical to other Mesopotamian myths where man is created from the earth. Woman is made from his rib as his helpmate and we're told that's why people get married. In the next chapter the Garden of Eden story gives explanations for why women have pain in childbirth, why farming is hard, and why snakes slither on their bellies. If I didn't know better I'd think these were supposed to be humorous stories akin to things parents tell their children like storks bring the babies kind of stuff.

"Paine it is simply rude and disrespectful to speak of God's word that way."

Nevertheless, millions of Christians view these stories as symbolic or representative of what ancient people believed about God, not as stories to be taken literally and certainly not as science.

"Millions of people might think they are Christians but if they do not believe the word of God they are destined for destruction. That's why we need to elect godly officials who will stand up for the truth and put the bible back in schools and in the government."

You really believe that don't you?

"Absolutely, Paine."

Separation of Church and State questions aside, I was wondering if you can defend your views based upon the actual contents of the bible. For example, the bible condones slavery. Slavery is illegal in the United States. The overwhelming majority of people believe it is immoral to own or even want to own other human beings. How can you justify using a book in government or public education that promotes enslaving people?

"That was a different time, Paine. Paul said if slaves could gain their freedom that was fine. Last time I looked they did. I will say that with all the people who live off the government check it might just be time to revisit certain bible passages."

Reverend, last time I looked politicians lived off the government check as well. Given the large number of them who believe their role is to do nothing beyond what big corporations and special interests want them to do maybe it is time to revisit a few passages in the constitution.

"Apples and oranges, Paine, apples and oranges."

Alright, what about genocide? You claim the god of the bible is a loving, moral, and compassionate god, yet on more than one occasion he commands the genocide and destruction of the cultures that occupied Canaan. For instance, in 1 Samuel King Saul was ordered to obliterate the Amalekites, every man, woman, child, infant, and even their animals. Not only is genocide illegal in the US, it is considered an egregious crime against humanity. How could you possibly advocate this kind of ethnocentrism and murder?

"Paine, those were different times. Today we await the Lord Jesus Christ who will judge the nations. Make no mistake about it. There will be a lot of death and destruction. But God's wrath is a righteous wrath and God's judgment cannot be questioned. Maybe people need to take a sober look at these stories and repent."

Out of fear?

"The fear of the Lord is the beginning of wisdom."

Does it concern you reverend that numerous times throughout history nations and empires have viewed these passages as a way to legitimize conquest and genocide? The claim that God is "on our side" has been used to justify some of the worst atrocities the world has ever seen. In fact isn't this exactly what Islamic extremists like ISIL are doing now?

"Those people are terrorists who believe in a false God. "

That's what they say about us. So to the victor goes the spoils, and credit to the god of the winners.

"It's not that simple, Paine. God makes nations rise and nations fall. Our nation may fall if Jesus Christ isn't firmly established as Lord and King. God led the way for the rise of our great country. He used our ancestors through crusades and conquests and heathen peoples who denied the authority of Christ fell by the way. This is all the more reason to put the bible back in schools and in government."

You honestly believe exposing children to stories of war, genocide, rape, murder, enslavement, and decimation of cultures is appropriate? The bible is full of these stories. I mean on what planet is it acceptable to expose children to a story like the rape of Dinah, the daughter of Jacob? She was taken forcibly by

Shechem and raped with the intention of forcing her to be his wife. Subsequently, the sons of Israel tricked the men of Shechem into being circumcised and while they were recovering slaughtered them. They murdered all of the men, took the women and children as slaves, and confiscated all of the Hivites animals and possessions. Not only is this story hideous and offensive on numerous levels, but it contradicts everything we believe to be just under a rule of law where each person is accountable for her or his own actions.

"Paine, I believe that story provides a good lesson about stirring up a hornet's nest. When you provoke the righteous then judgment comes. Besides, the people of Shechem were not God's chosen people."

They had it coming.

"I believe they did."

The bible makes lots of provisions for capital punishment. Nations that serve other gods are to be enslaved or annihilated. Men and women who cheat on their spouses are guilty of adultery and are to be put to death. People who use divination or consult mediums are to be executed. That means every American who reads a horoscope, uses a Ouija board, consults a psychic, or even people of Wiccan and Pagan faiths should be put to death. Children who rebel against their parents are to be put to death. The list could continue. The idea of punishing people in the United States for any of these things is illegal let alone administering capital punishment. There is even a great debate as to whether we should use capital punishment at all for even the most heinous crime, so how can you justify the exaltation of ancient religious and cultural law codes that are considered unconstitutional and barbaric?

"Like I've already said God is a righteous judge and many people will suffer for the things they do. We might not be able to put all of these laws into effect, but with the bible at the forefront we can at least teach and warn people of what they have coming."

But if you could, would you advocate enforcing biblical laws?

"Well, I'm a Christian and I believe all laws should be viewed through Christ. These things are sins and shouldn't be taken lightly. People shouldn't commit adultery, read horoscopes, and children should respect their parents."

And if a child has ADHD or Tourette syndrome which are among the illnesses that have symptoms that could be interpreted as rebellion, what then? One has to wonder if the ignorance of ancient people led to the execution of children that needed treatment instead of punishment. Even modern parents who follow certain bible teachings use corporal punishment when medical or psychological alternatives are the viable solution.

"I don't know Paine, there's a lot to be said for 'Spare the rod, and spoil the child.' A lot of these kids today could use a trip out to the woodshed."

I remember a fellow telling me a story once about his preacher who was in the middle of a sermon when some rowdy youth were disrupting the service. The exasperated preacher said to the congregation "If I can't preach heaven into 'em, I'm going to beat hell out of 'em," and proceeded to leave the pulpit to do just that.

"Oh I like that one Paine."

I thought you would. So Reverend Twinger without doubt the bible is laden with stories of horrific violence, war, assassinations, even genocide. Some stories are quite grotesque like the woman Jael driving a tent peg through Sisera's head while he slept. There is Ehud the left-handed Benjaminite who assassinates Eglon the fat Moabite king while he is on his toilet, and the men of Gibeah who raped a man's concubine to death. The man cuts her up into twelve pieces and sends her body parts to the tribes as a call for vengeance. All this said, most Christians seem to interpret their faith as a religion of love and peace. Jesus is frequently depicted as a pacifist, one who teaches passive resistance over violence, and one who taught love for enemies even to the point of self-sacrifice. I have to say I'm a little confused as to why those of you who are the most conservative, letter of the law, stick to the bible, seem to be pro-gun, pro-death penalty, pro-war, but yet against health care for all and programs that reduce the hardships of poverty. How do you respond to this?

"Paine, Jesus never said his people couldn't defend themselves. It is our right as Christians and as Americans to bear arms and defend the principles we hold dear. As far as I'm concerned God and guns goes hand in hand. Now if the people on drugs and welfare lived right, worked jobs like they ought to, then they wouldn't be asking for handouts from hard working righteous people. "

Just let them "die and decrease the surplus population."

"Well sin and sloth has its consequences. Tribulation is coming. It's the word of God. I'll tell you straight up, when sin comes knocking on my door, it's gonna eat lead."

Rev. Twinger, no offense, but you scare the hell out of me. That should make you happy.

"Whatever works, Paine."

Reverend we've covered a lot of ground. You make it clear that you want the bible to be the centerpiece of American life. It should influence government and be taught in public schools. You don't have a problem with the many laws that are contradicted and rendered illegal by the US constitution, and you don't seem to mind the idea that children would potentially be exposed to the violence contained in many passages. Before we conclude tonight's interview I want to ask you about the sex mentioned in many bible stories. Do you really believe this is appropriate for children?

"Paine you'd have to be specific, but I'm not aware of anything in God's word that is not appropriate for children."

Song of Songs. It almost didn't make it into the Hebrew canon because of its erotic symbolism. It's in the bible because some priests and rabbis took it to be an allegory for God's love for Israel. I mean what about these verses? "I had put off my garment…My beloved thrust his hand into the opening, and my inmost being yearned for him. I arose to open for my beloved, and my hand dripped with myrrh, my fingers with liquid myrrh, upon the handles of the bolt." Or "Your channel is an orchard of pomegranates, with all choicest fruits … Blow upon my garden that its fragrance may be wafted abroad. Let my beloved come to his garden, and eat its choicest fruits." This is just a taste reverend from this text. What's a teacher going to say when students ask about what it means? Is there going to be an explanation of foreplay, intercourse, fellatio, cunnilingus?

"I don't know where you get your interpretations there Paine, but I have never thought about it that way."

Have you ever even thought about it?

"It's not exactly the most important book of the bible, and I rather doubt a teacher would teach from it anyway."

How do you know that? That's a huge problem. Public school teachers are not clergy, they are not trained bible scholars, and the biases of different denominations are all over the map. There's no accountability whatsoever. Any passage from the bible whether it contained violence or sex or whatever could be presented to students at the whim of the teacher and interpreted by her or his opinion.

"I don't really think it matters Paine. The word of God speaks for itself. When people hear it the inspiration of God's spirit is there to guide them."

Really? So how would you explain this to a classroom of students? I alluded to it earlier. Genesis 6 says "The Nephilim were on the earth in those days, and also afterward, when the sons of El went in to the daughters of humans, who bore children to them. These were the heroes that were of old, warriors of renown." This is the beginning of the Flood story. It suggests a time when gods were having sex with mortal women which led to half god-half mortal beings like Gilgamesh, Hercules, etc. It ends with El being disgusted with the corruption and violence of it all and the decision to destroy every living thing except eight people and a boat load of animals.

"Paine, the problem here is you are not a Christian. You cannot understand the word of God because you do not believe it by faith. I do not do bible study with unbelievers. But taught correctly by godly teachers there's a lot in this story worth learning."

So you want to impose your theology and views of the bible on everyone else, but for those of us that have questions that's tough because we do not share your interpretations or believe the way you do?

"What's right is right is right."

Ok, here's a passage that doesn't need much explanation. Deuteronomy 22:28 states "If a man meets a virgin who is not engaged, and seizes her and lies with her, and they are caught in the act, the man who lay with her shall give fifty shekels of silver to the young woman's father, and she shall become his wife." Not only does this law legitimize rape, and devalue women as mere property, but it implies there is only a penalty if the guy gets caught. Would you want your daughter to learn this story in public school? Wouldn't a story like this only encourage boys to think they could get away with date rape? This is as horrible as it is illegal.

"Those times are in the past now Paine. We read these passages through the law of Christ, but again you'd have to be a believer to understand that."

As a Christian fundamentalist you take the story of the virgin birth of Jesus literally.

"Yes, Paine, I certainly do."

The verses here in Deuteronomy that precede the one I just read say if the virgin the man lies with is engaged to be married to someone else he is to be put to death and if she doesn't yell for help during the rape she too must die. In Luke's gospel and a little less specific in Matthew God chooses to impregnate Mary, a virgin engaged to Joseph, with his divine issue. Isn't that a violation and blatant contradiction with God's own law? It also seems to be the very thing that God used as a pretext to deluge the earth in the Genesis passage I read. How is this a moral story suitable for children and doesn't it set a double standard? God seems to be a being that can do as he pleases – Do as I say, not as I do.

"God can do any and everything he sees fit to bring about the manifestation of his will, but I resent the implication that God is a rapist and adulterer. We're talking about the Lord Jesus Christ, Son of the Living God, and Savior of the world."

Well reverend what's right is right is right, huh. And if the shoe fits, which it seems to, you have to wear it.

"If you were a Christian, you'd understand, and you certainly wouldn't question the will of God."

My questions are for you reverend. You are the one who wants this bible which you claim is the perfect, inerrant, inspired word of God to influence government and be taught in schools. Would you want to be the parent of little Johnny or Susie who comes home from school after hearing the story of Onan in the book of Genesis? You remember that one don't you reverend? You know, Onan's brother was dead and Onan was supposed to have sex with his late brother's wife to produce offspring on his brother's behalf. But every time he has sex with her he pulls his penis out of her vagina and masturbates his semen onto the ground. Then God strikes him dead for it.

"Onan did what was evil in the sight of the Lord and was rightly punished. That's the moral lesson to learn. And frankly Paine, the bible doesn't say penis, vagina, or masturbate."

Do you think children are stupid?

"Know I'm sure they're not, but properly taught they learn respect and to fear the Lord."

And what do they learn from this story reverend? In Genesis 19 after the destruction of Sodom and Gomorrah Lot and his two daughters are living in a cave. The girls express their concerns to each other that they will not find husbands so they conspire to take turns getting their father drunk to have sex with him. They do this. First one then the other, and they become pregnant.

"I don't think a teacher would use this story, but it does make a good case for abstinence."

Come on reverend, sometimes I get the feeling that your ideology about the bible has blinded you to what's actually in it. If you are paying attention to the story don't you at least pause to get a mental picture of what's going on? I mean how is it in a day without Viagra that a drunken old man is going to get it up? Did he get on them in a lustful stupor and forget the next day what he had done or did they wait till he passed out and get on him? What kind of sex acts would be involved in something like that? Did they masturbate him and fellate him first or what? Do you not think these things are going to occur to kids, especially teenagers, boys giggling with crude innuendos in the hallways after class?

"Paine this is a story in the word of God and it is there because it is true and for a reason."

Let me suggest to you what it is and why it is there. The children born to the daughters were Moab and Ammon, two rival clans of the Israelites. The story is there as an ethnic slur about on par with any racist story in any culture. It's an inbred hillbilly story, a disgusting story fabricated in racial prejudice. At least that's how it comes across to me, and I think it strains credulity to believe that any of these ancient stories and law codes has any place in American government or public education.

"As I wrote in my book, Paine, what's right is
right is right, unless it is wrong, and I believe you are
wrong. God's word is always right."

Reverend Twinger you can think what you want,
but I'll tell you this; these stories are just a few
examples of the sex and macabre practices mentioned
in the bible. If I collected the bible stories that contain
what is clearly adult oriented material and put them
together as a collection without the title "Bible" on it
and disseminated it to minors I'd be arrested for a sex
crime.

"Well Paine, maybe you should just leave the
bible to those of us that believe its truth, and let us
worry about what is taught, and what applies to law
and moral living. You clearly don't get it. But Paine I
just want you to know I love you in the Lord. Before I
leave here tonight I want to give you a chance that's
worth more than gold. I invite you to accept the Lord
Jesus Christ as your personal savior, have your sins
all washed away, and be saved. "

If I did that reverend are you saying the bible
would suddenly make sense to me?

"Like an infant that first has to nurse from its
mother, all babes in Christ begin slowly. In Jesus you
can trust us to explain it to you."

Ladies and gentlemen, that's my guest for the
evening, the Reverend R. I. Twinger. Rev. Twinger's
new book is What's Right is Right is Right, Unless It's

Wrong. Thank you Reverend for joining us on this week's edition of Common Sense.

"Thank you Paine for helping me get the word out. It has been my pleasure."

Tonight we have heard the views of Reverend R.I. Twinger. Clearly he represents a significant population of fundamentalist Christians that includes many prominent politicians. For them the bible supersedes constitutional law, and their agenda is to implement various standards from the bible they choose to be relevant for today's society. But is this a moral agenda. While many believe the bible to be about love, acceptance, and compassion, it does contain a substantive amount of material of a questionable nature. There is the violence and sex. There is incest and rape. There are the passages that condone genocide, slavery, racism, discrimination, homophobia, polygamy, the subjugation of women to the status of property, and of course capital punishment for a whole slew of people including rebellious children. It may be that through reason, science, and a more fine tuned understanding of humanity we have evolved beyond these artifacts of an ancient culture. Is it possible that society is more decent and moral, just and fair, without the bible? Perhaps not, at least that has been Rev. R.I. Twinger's point of view. His agenda is out there. It is on the move. As always I leave it to you to decide. As he says, "What's right is right is right, unless it is wrong.

Join us in the coming weeks when our guests will include Supreme Court justice Clarence Thomas where we will discuss the days when SCOTUS redefined marriage to include interracial couples and Gov. Mike Huckabee's recent remarks about Dread Scott. We have Sarah Palin coming to discuss the American language she believes all should speak. Does she mean the polished grammar of formal English or the more hybridized colloquial speech laden with cliché and generalization that is widely popular among conservatives like her? Of course she could have meant Native American. We'll find out. And you certainly won't want to miss next week's show with Donald Trump. We'll talk walls, big walls. We'll find out why it wouldn't be easier to simply improve U.S. bureaucratic infrastructure to better incorporate migrant workers. There does seem to be more jobs available to migrant families than the number we currently allow for legal immigration. We'll ask the savvy business mogul why it wouldn't be more lucrative to invest in Mexico and Latin American countries to create more jobs there and help bring their labor and wage standards in line with our own. Could such a strategy solve the immigration crisis without deporting eleven million hard working people and blocking the view across the Rio Grande? DT will know.

To date we've had no luck with invitations we've sent to Senators Cruz, Paul, and others to join us on Common Sense. We've been told their schedules will not permit the time for it. As always our commitment is to do the very best to bring on the guests you want to hear, so keep tuning in and follow us on social media for all the latest commentary. If someone is saying it, we'll be giving it the ol' cognitive whirl. This is Common Sense, and I'm your host, Paine Thomas.

CPSIA information can be obtained at www.ICGtesting.com
Printed in the USA
LVOW11*1608171015

458279LV00003BA/21/P